AF432722

ALSO BY BARNABAS SMITH

PAPERBACK
Circles All the Way Down, 2020
The Stories We Tell Ourselves, 2019
Movement & Repose, 2012

CHAPBOOK
Serenade the Fire, 2020
ANYWHERE, 2018
Vagabond Doctrine, 2013
Things Not Yet, 2006

Circles All the Way Down

Barnabas Smith

A FISTFUL OF WORDS 2023

For Theodore & Ollivander

*You inspire me everyday as you trace my circles
and venture to make your own*

TEACHER:
What is the nature of reality?

STUDENT:
It is circles, all the way down.

CONTENTS

ANYWHERE

ANYWHERE

1

I'll take you anywhere you want to go
Name the time and place
Dream big, don't hesitate
Don't get distracted by details
Whether we'll be back in time
For less spontaneous endeavors
How we will fill our plates
How we will spend our days
Anywhere means anywhere
I'll take you there

2

He never travels anywhere
Without his camera
Snapshots of the world
Moments frozen in time
The cosmos in a frame
Preserved in photograph
Their appearance
Perhaps their names
Perhaps their pain
He is never found without his camera
He is never found without
He is never found

3

There are no reserved seats
Just sit anywhere you like
Buckle up, adjust your seat
Keep your arms inside
Can't promise a smooth ride
Can't promise we'll be on time
Can't promise you I'm alright
(Promises are made
Out of flimsy convictions
Seated without reservation)

4

The only one who's anywhere
Close to the truth is my mother
And that may or may not
Have to do with the fact
That from her womb
I gained life and light and
So much more than existence
From her breast came
Sustenance and comfort and
So much more than innocence
My mother is closer to anywhere
Than truth be told

ANYWHERE

5

I was wondering if
There was anywhere
I could go to get this repaired
It broke into a million pieces
Crushed under the weight
Of too much pressure
Of too much expectation
And not enough hope
Is there anywhere
I could go to get this repaired
My heart

6

He could get anywhere
From three to seven years
Behind bars built
From the ruins of his life
Forged in the fires of failure
Walls constructed from
The bricks of ill intent
Locked with the key
Of misguided youth
With a window letting in
Rays of hope and
A song of liberation

7

There are plants in this desert
That you won't find anywhere else
They thrive in harsh conditions
Grow through lack of water and
Overabundance of sunlight
The heat of the day
Does not dry up their hope
They are resilient
There are plants elsewhere
That cannot survive
The desert

8

He seems to be at home
Anywhere in the world
Except in places where
He must wear a mask
Speak words not his own
Strive toward goals
He does not own
Holding on to memories
Of a place once known
As home
Now known as
Anywhere

9

The attack could come
From anywhere and that
Was the most mundane
Aspect of this scenario
The fascinating thing was
That after ten years at war
She had never seen the enemy
Only people defending
The very same things
She was

10

You'll never get anywhere
With that attitude
My mother would say
A resounding voice in my head
Disembodied from her gentle touch
Years removed from her last breath
One of many phrases floating
Like bottles tossed into the sea
Of my memory seeking to be read

ANYWHERE

11

I wouldn't dream
Of letting a surgeon
Anywhere near my eyes
They are the gateways
To the multiverse inside of me
My iris, a nebula of stardust
My pupil, an event horizon
To infinite constellations
Orbiting the nexus of my reality
I fear that all of this might ruin
The surgeon

12

Does my answer come
Anywhere near the right one?
Does my demeanor convey
The emotional gravity
I am trying to muster?
Do my words match the
Seriousness of the situation?
Or did I, like so many other times,
Answer from a place of hostility
Defending a moment anywhere
But now

13

Imitations rarely look
Anywhere near as good
As the real thing
They are close enough
To fool most at first glance
Those too consumed by fear
To stop and inspect for themselves
They trust the mirage
Drink sand for fear of thirst
While springs of freedom
Go unnoticed

14

We're not anywhere near
To being finished
We've only just begun
See the door wide open
See the walls coming down
See the footprints of those
Charging on before us
Follow the footprints
Tear down the walls
Fling wide the door
We've only just begun

15

I could go anywhere
In the world
That place would be home
The atomic makeup
Of the cosmos
Is contained within me
We are alone together
Bound by the same
Spark of eternity
Standing on the
Threshold of infinity
At home wherever
We allow ourselves
To be

BEYOND

BEYOND

1

We could see the valley
And the hills beyond
Our hearts swelled with
The joy of anticipation
The expectation of beauty
We momentarily forgot
Ourselves and our place
In the world, we wanted
What was beyond our sight

2

He pointed to a spot
Beyond the trees
On the horizon
Spoke of distant shores
Of sea monsters
Of trade winds
Of ocean currents
He pointed to another spot
Beyond the horizon
He asked for my thoughts
But I was stuck in a trance
Watching the passion
On his lips

3

Beyond the river
Was a small town
Constructed out of flotsam
Washed upon the shore
Carefully reassembled
Renewed into habitats
For outcast inhabitants
Of a broken kingdom
With shipwrecks in their soul
And a desire to keep course
Regardless of the storms
Or vicissitudes of time

4

She has changed beyond recognition
It started with small things
Deconstructing one wall at a time
Facades replaced by mosaics
Of broken glass and metal
Salvaged from the jetsam in her soul
Held together with intentionality
Welded by the fires of renewal
Rising from her own ashes

5

There was little vegetation
Beyond brush-growth
Soil reduced to dirt
Its biome bereft of
Thriving microbes and other
Organisms needed for larger plants
To take root and thrive
Providing cover for
Brush-growth to thrive
Connected circle
Always turning
Always turning
Always turning

6

The world beyond the prison wall
Was beginning to fade away
After a decade, memories became
Legends in her mind
Stories of her life outside
Took their place alongside
Alice, Harry, and the others
Lifetimes internalized like a lifeboat
In the cold dark alone
She now found herself

7

The situation is already
Beyond our control
All we can do now is breathe

Breathe in the universe
Let it fill your chest cavity
Let if fill your blood cells
Let it fill you until
You exhale stardust
And speak in languages
Long since forgotten to time

Wholeness
Oneness
Thisness
Hereness

Inhale the cosmos
Exhale humanity

8

Their relationship was
Strained beyond the breaking point
Caused by too many broken promises
Affected by too many hollow words
Weighed down by too much pressure
From the outside
From the inside
From each other
Until it formed something new
Like a diamond turning in the light

9

They heard footsteps
In the main room, beyond a door
They heard breathing
In the kitchen, below the floor
They were alone for the night
But weren't alone anymore
They were alone with their crime
Until he opened the door

10

She asked for nothing
Beyond peace and quiet
When it came it felt like
A room of busy children
Suddenly leaving a crowded room
A wave upon a shore
Rushing out to the horizon
She became shrouded in
The peace of chaos
The stillness of the noise
The movement of repose

11

Just beyond the fence
Is a world full of wonder
Full of joy unfathomable
Waiting to be experienced
Interacted with
Enjoyed without restraint
The secret to getting
Across the fence is
Realizing we experience only
What we allow
Ourselves to see

12

I cannot plan beyond tomorrow
For tomorrow has little to do
With my current capacity
To envision what today might be
For today is enough on its own
Without trying to take into account
Whether a butterfly will flap its wings
Or if Saturn will hold its rings

13

We can't see beyond ourselves
When we are consumed
By ourselves
When we are consumed
By the flames of a hell
Of our own making
When we clinch our eyes shut
For fear of being confronted
With the unpleasant reality
That there is suffering
Anywhere beyond ourselves

BEYOND

14

An evil beyond remedy
Resides in the corner of our minds
Lurking, stalking, waiting
For a moment of weakness
When it can cause the most division
When it can speak the best lie
When it can twist the thoughts
Within the corner of our minds
Turn us against our neighbor
Against the world
Against ourselves

15

Beyond midnight
Is the dawn of a new day
New opportunities
Beyond new horizons
Moments never experienced
Mistakes not yet made
Lessons not yet learned
Suffering yet to give birth
To new ways of seeing the world
Pulling us closer
Pulling us deeper
Into the divine
And each other

OURSELVES

1

We may be deceiving ourselves
To think that now
Is so different from then
To believe that now has never been
And will never be again
There has always been empires
Has always been oppressed
But also
Those that transcend
Bringing then into now
And not yet into existence

2

We couldn't see ourselves
In the photograph
Time had passed too hard
Since that moment was exposed
Since that moment became frozen
In time and put on display
We couldn't remember the last time
Genuine smiles graced our faces
We couldn't see ourselves
We were no longer there

3

We built this ourselves
With tired hands
And tired hearts
We brought together
All we could muster
In hopes that
In the age to come
Our lives would be our legacy
The foundation for a new world

4

We are ourselves when we're together
No shroud of deception between us
No need for first impressions
Or to be impressive
All of us started somewhere else
Now we are here and are going there
And that is all that matters
The prologue to our shared journey
Is diverse but not divisive
But our goals are all the same

5

We really enjoyed ourselves
Dancing under starlight
Turning in orbits around each other
Colliding and creating new bodies
Drifting and duplicating bodies
We moved in patterns only gravity
Could permit
In ways that only physics
Could predict
We wished this moment
Was permanent

6

We're feeling ourselves again
It's taken some time but
We are here now
Present
Aware
Fully aware of our presence
How we are so much more
Than protons and electrons
Than pronouns and elections
We are beyond ourselves

7

We saw ourselves in the mirror
At first, we could not believe
The prominence of our flaws
The ways in which our bodies failed
Ways in which we were
Less than our desires
Our eyes turned toward each other
And then
Our desires turned with them

8

We were talking among ourselves
It sounded like an echo
Bouncing off the walls of a cave
Agreement and disagreement
Ceased to exist in the void
Of our self-affirmation
A bass note hummed from
The center of the universe
Inviting us into conversation
But we dared not leave the cave

9

We'll just have to finish
The job ourselves
No one will do it for us
We are no longer willing
To let this question linger
No longer willing to give our lives
While you search for an answer
You sharpen the claws
To tame the lion
We say enough

10

We should not compare ourselves
To the ones who are stuck
In a fortress of their own making
Or to the ones who are so far ahead
They have lost sight of the tribe
We are a different sort
Using the past as foundation
For future constructs
Oscillating between
Priesthood and prophecy

11

We cannot trust ourselves
To keep our lenses clear
Without having a way to clean them
They will build up with dust
And grime and oils
Until all we can see is what
We hope to see
Or hope not to see
Our vision becomes distorted
By the biases in our heads
With no light coming in
Our eyes grow dim
Blinded by our own selves

12

Come, let us comfort
Ourselves with love
Let us have our fill of it
Until morning comes
And a new day dawns
Then let us fill ourselves again
Until we overflow with the
Boundless energy of the universe
Drifting around each other
Taking care of our neighbors
Anywhere they might be

13

We should keep this to ourselves
This kind of thing should be
Kept under wraps
A secret among friends
A legend among a tribe
No one should know
That we possess the power
Of the cosmos
Within the core of our being
Imagine if they knew

14

We locked ourselves out
And while it was embarrassing
It was not the height of folly
Since there was no door
And thus no lock
We were kept from entering
A space of our own making
Blocked by the shortcomings
Of our thinking
And our desire to enter
Despite there not being a door

15

Let's stop talking about ourselves
Lest we start believing our own lies
Leading us to drastic actions
Let's try something new
Let's be quiet for a while
Let's close up shop
Open ourselves up to the invitation
To just be, while the universe
Breathes life into our tired lungs

16

We enjoy ourselves
On Saturday mornings
The week's chaos now quiet
The coming days before us
Full of hope and joy
Despite the walls coming down
We have each other
Will always have each other
To be the anchor and the sail

ANCHOR & SAIL

1

We lost our anchor
Which caused the boat to drift
For a moment we panicked
No land in sight
No stars to give us bearing
No wind to fill the sail
As the sky grew dim
The waves rocked us
We drifted off to sleep
With no anchor to reality

2

The sails billowed
With the breeze they caught
We began to move
The waves beat against us
The sun behind us
We made our way home
Sails full of wind
Hearts full of hope

3

His fear anchored him
Not the kind that paralyzes
But the kind that drives a wedge
Into the core of your being
Invites you to dive into the depths
Of the cavern it has made
Rest in the unknowing
Contemplate the darkness
And become one with yourself

4

We sail at dawn
Toward distant shores
Beyond the edges of our maps
Toward places uncharted
Through unknown seas
Under unknown constellations
With nothing to hold us back
But our own hesitation

5

Her memories anchored her
To her hometown
Vivid images of past experiences
Replaying like the second run
Of an old sitcom
She knew all of the jokes
All of the quirks
All of the hidden facts
Yet still, she would not return
For the next season

6

The ball sailed over the fence
Into the yard of an old man
Reminiscent of a cyclops
Whose house was rumored
To be a point of entry for
Demons and other evil things
No ball ever came back
No boy ever dared to go
Into the wild unknown
Over the fearful fence
But she didn't care

7

Religion was his anchor
It gave him a center to orbit
A place of refuge in the storm
Words of comfort during hard times
Guidelines for living a holy life
Religion was his god
It gave him distraction from his life
Something to hide behind
It kept the divine at a distance

8

The day sailed by
Like paper boats down a stream
Rushed about by currents
Carried far away from their
Point of origin
As children chase them
Cheer for near misses
Jump with all the excitement
Of not knowing
Of being unfazed by
The passage of time

9

The rock provided
An anchor for the rope
As they started to drift away
Made buoyant by their hope
As their souls rose
To higher planes of excellence
Their physical bodies followed suit
Causing friends to tether them
With cord and line and facts
How misguided

10

We sailed through customs
After twenty-four hours in the air
Seventeen hours on a bus
And three months away
We changed somewhere between
Leaving and coming back
Arriving at customs to enter
The country of our birth
But not the one we call home

11

He anchored his life in Wisdom
For She never steered him wrong
Living life based on ancient words
Concepts bigger than himself
What worried him was when
After Wisdom's tender kiss
She would whisper
There is more than just me
There are lessons to be learned
That only you can teach

12

The earth sails through space
At thirty kilometers a second
The billions of people
Living on its surface
Are made up of the same
Ratio of elements
As the planet they share
[Which moves and shakes
At the same rate our
Fingernails grow]
Yet they are skeptical
Of the significance

13

Two major stores once anchored
Each end of the shopping mall
That now sits dormant
Like the carcass of a dragon
Once consuming visitors
As they shopped for things
They did not need
At the same time
Providing jobs they did need
Now doing neither
Just lying there
A vacant memorial

14

Sail on past the sharks
Sail on past the crags
Sail on past the storm
Lest they sink you
Consume energy
Better spent elsewhere
Sail on toward new horizons
Sail on toward distant shores
Sail on toward better days
Sail on

15

The roots of the tree
Are anchored deep
Into the soil by a river
That flows into the sea

Its limbs and leaves
Reach out to pull in
Carbon and sunlight
To create life using
The refuse of the cosmos

SACRED

SACRED

1

Make it sacred
This moment
This place
This time we find
Ourselves faced with
Unending possibilities
Opportunities to share
The story that is within
The essence of our being
Holding us together
Like a bundle of wood
Ready to start a fire

2

We made a temporary wall
To protect ourselves
Not realizing that
Keeping things out
Meant keeping things in
The pressure ruptured the barrier
The river overran its banks
Washing away all division
Bringing all things into
Its watery embrace

3

When I look into your eyes
I see worlds of endless
Ever expanding possibilities
For you
For me
You are the multiverse incarnate
Welcoming me into
The black holes of your eyes
Consuming and synthesizing
Better versions of ourselves
Made from the inmost center
Of us

4

In the beginning
The universe birthed itself
By folding in on itself
By expanding itself
Holding the tension
Between chaos and order
Between growth and decay
And so shall you, my child
So shall you

5

The Name of all things
Spoken before sound
Known before knowing
Quantumly entangled
With the Eternal
Moves like a song
Through the cosmos
A bass note resounding
All the way down
All the way down
All the way down

6

The Voice called out
        Speak to the children
        Tell them of the mystery
        The oscillation between
        Movement and stillness
        Throughout the cosmos
        From quark to galaxies
        All things violently born
        All things given rest
        Before they give birth
        All things becoming new

7

In the wilderness
The Voice speaks
    Count your offspring
    Number your generations
    See your creations
    For what they are
    Sparks of the Infinite
    Surrounding you
    Reflecting my goodness
    Back to you
    Calling you to stillness
    And movement
    In sync with the cosmos

8

These are the words
That bare witness to
Knowing and unknowing
The ongoing collision of
Matter and spirit
The centering of ourselves
In rhythm with the cosmos
Igniting the potential within
To further love in dormant places
Until we return
To stardust and energy

9

You unravel me
Then knit me back together
Filling me with more
Reminding me that I am more
That I am We
You and I and others
In this together
You unravel Us
Then knit Us back together

10

I am a wandering star
You cannot be eclipsed
I cannot resist your gravity
I am made of galaxies
My composition the same
As solar systems
I contain the cosmos within me
Am contained within the cosmos
A covenant of matter and spirit
Looking to connect
To the source of every good

11

The resurrection is a testament
To the power of love to create life
in the midst of chaos and death
It is the first word of creation
Spoken again
It is an invitation
To throw off the shackles of Babylon
To throw down the weapons of Rome
To seek first the Kingdom of God

12

How do we speak of
This oneness
This unity of spirit
This rhythmic entanglement
Two becoming one
Two becoming one
Two becoming one
One becoming

What the Divine has joined
Let no one try to separate
This circle dance of
Trust, desire, and passion

13

The landscape begs
To be lived in
The woods ask
To be explored
The water reflects
Our distorted images
Image bearers interacting
With the cosmos
Discovering our place
Within the vast wilderness
Finding rest and a steady rhythm
Among the evergreens
And creeping things

14

There is a star in the distance
Guiding all to the center
As we circle the Source
It encourages all to come
To shed every excess
And focus on the One
But as the way with all stars
The light we see has already shone
The messenger already gone
Yet lives on always guiding us home

CIRCLES

1

A circle of dancers
In rhythmic unison
May vary in their movement
Some jump
Some spin
Some shake
Yet all are in the same dance
one shared choreography
One shared heartbeat

2

He spun her into the air
Like a pair of swing dancers
Only, he held her arms
Behind her back
Only, her feet never
Returned to the ground
Instead, it was her face
That met the sacred earth
His fear desecrating
The image of the Divine
While Rachel mourns
And Christ weeps

3

He circled the house cautiously
Unsure of what would happen
If he approached unannounced
Would he startle the occupants
Were they home
Did he want them to be
He had been gone
For far too long
Or had he
Space-time is not so easily
Understood

4

She moved only in
The most exalted circles
Preferring the company of power
To the dread of suffering
That ever-present companion
Constantly by her side

She escapes
To high and lofty places
Trusting distance to be a remedy
But the pain is always there

5

She flicked the spinner
And watched as the wings
Became one multicolored swirl
One unified motion
Each taking the place of the other
Like holding a galaxy in her palm
Or viewing an atom
Or the way she loved her wife
Each taking the place of the other
One unified motion

6

The halos around their heads
Are to show us that they were
Chosen by the Divine
To perform miracles
And do great things
But the whole thing is a miracle
The cosmos, the earth, and you
Every act of love, great
Every one of us, chosen
Filled with divine light
Living with unseen halos

7

A ball of flame in the sky
Gives energy as it decays
Its life-giving essence
Concurrent with its demise

We consume that energy
In a plethora of ways
We are made up of
A multitude of flames

8

The annual rings speak to us
Each one tells their own story
Each one hides their own secrets
Each circle, a line of poetry
Together forming an epic
Declaring a life spent navigating
Abundance and drought
Ended by the swift action
Of an ax whose handle
Was once apart of this tree

9

The wheels turn
The world turns
As I become one
With the cadence
Of my pedals

I breathe in light
Exhale darkness
Both momentarily
Contained within me
As I ride down the path
Becoming aware of
The Presence within
This particular here
And this eternal now

10

A small circle of friends
Sitting around a table
Sharing stories of the past
Sharing dreams for the future
Enjoying the now they share
Is how every good movement starts
With power in their midst
United for justice through love
Turning the world upside down

11

Rainbows are circles of light
Yet we rarely see
The full circumference
Often obscured by the horizon
Or our vantage point
But the circle is always there
Despite how we view it
Light is not dependent
Upon our seeing to shine

12

If your eye is good
You will see reality
As it was meant to be seen
With the same eye
That the Infinite sees

Curiosity and compassion
Will guide you into love
And eradicate all fear
Allowing you to see beyond
Yourself into a new reality

13

Bullet holes act as punctuation
   Full stop
They are the response
   To a plea
They are the answer
   To a question
Often they are the exclamation
   Of fear and frustration
Finding their way into
Someone even more afraid
A life now ended with
   A colon, period, dot dot dot

14

Love is the compass
That guides us into the unknown
Further down the unfolding path
Away from and beyond ourselves
Into participation with the ongoing
Renewal of all things

15

And the clock struck nine
The chime sounding out
Through the hall
Followed by a silence
That broke like waves
Upon a twilight threshold
Beyond which
Darkness and stillness
Invited all to rest from
The movement of time

16

A blue dot in a sea of endless light
Spinning in galactic tides
Bathed in cosmic energy
Dancing with others
Around a dying star
The same way
We dance when
The energy of our being
Exceeds words or feeling
Despite the circumstances
We know this will always be home

17

The lioness circled her prey
The gazelles eyed their predator
They engaged in a dance
That goes back thousands of years
Ensuring the survival of both
Through the death of one
Comes the life of the other
When the prey is caught
Or when the predator starves
The dance goes on and on

18

The record spins and the music plays
The sounds of a jazz band float
Through the room and into my soul
Lifting me with every note played
Moving me with every kick
Giving me room to meditate
As the world fades into
Harmony and silence

19

The moonrise was breathtaking
Its soft glow touching everything

How long will we stand here, I asked

As long as it takes for us
to become one, You replied

Hugging me tighter
Your head tucked under my chin

Like the sun and moon,
you added with a sigh

Which one am I, I thought

20

His circles are not circles
But they are perfect
A snapshot of his imagination
Captured in colored wax
Smooshed on paper
His chosen medium
Multicolored expressions
Of childlike wonder
And explorations
His lines are not straight
But they are perfect
Connecting his heart to mine

FREEDOM

FREEDOM

I

They were given their freedom
All chains and burdens gone
All whips and sticks laid down
All fences and walls torn down
They were allowed to go wherever
Their spirits or desires guided
In exchange for forgetting
All that had occurred
But they could not
And neither will we

II

They told me that freedom
Was not free, that someone died
So that I could enjoy America
But they did not tell me
Of those who died
Between the Continent
    and America
By whips and beatings
    in America
Or of those who died fighting
Against my freedom
In America
Freedom must forget

FREEDOM

III

It is a form of collective
Amnesia, this forgetting
Of events and conditions
For which we bore witness
The bodies pinned against
Brick walls by water
Or officers of the law
Bodies still drop to the ground
The blood flows and then dries
How quickly we trust
the promise of freedom

Notes

This collection of poetry started as a challenge to myself. It was sparked by cryptic tweets sent out by Shia LaBeouf via @thecampaignbook in February of 2018. These one-line statements begged for a response and so a challenge was born. I would respond to each one with a poem that fits within Twitter's new 280 character limit. As the tweets came, my response would soon come.

It was new territory for me and I loved it.

During these poetic responses, I discovered that these mysterious statements were being sourced from thefreedictionary.com. I used this knowledge to extend these poems past the initial ANYWHERE statements to form a small trilogy, ANYWHERE BEYOND OURSELVES.

After the trilogy was complete, I sent the manuscript off to various people and publishers.

No one bit and now you hold my resistance in your hands.

While I spent two years shopping out the manuscript, I continued to write within the Twitter limitations using various prompts and ideas. Some from the dictionary. Some from scripture, some from observations.

I would like to thank the various people who engaged with the initial poems, and those that followed, both on Twitter and on Instagram. Too many to name and more than I could hope. Years later and I still get notifications on some of those first poems

ANYWHERE was released as a digital chapbook, along with ANCHOR & SAIL (released as The Anchor & the Sail), and SACRED (released as Make It Sacred). Thank you to those who downloaded and read those small collections.

Poetry, well, writing in general, is often a solitary practice. I deeply enjoy the small band of followers I have acquired and interacted with the past few years. I look forward to many more.

I appreciate you and all that you do.

A note on Shia LaBeouf:
Since the initial printing of this collection a few things about Shia's personal life have come to light.

The details are everywhere so I don't have anything to add to the discourse.

I only have this to say.

I read an interview Shia did in 2007 around the release of the first Transformers movie. He was distant and lost. We are the same age so I felt somewhat connected. My hope for him then is the same it is now.

Shia,
May you surround yourself with good people
And find your way back to joy
No one is beyond returning to love
And setting right what they made wrong

Index

OURSELVES

ANCHOR & SAIL

SACRED

About the Author

Barnabas Smith is a poet, illustrator, and designer born and raised in Southern California. He has independently released four collections of poetry. He currently resides in Colorado with his two sons.